INDEPENDENCE

Andrew Motion was born in 1952 and educated at University College, Oxford. From 1977-1980 he was a lecturer in English at the University of Hull. He now lives and works in Oxford. He has published one collection of poems, *The Pleasure Steamers*, for which he received a Cholmondeley Award, and a critical book, *The Poetry of Edward Thomas*. In 1981 he won the Arvon/Observer Poetry Prize.

INDEPENDENCE

Andrew Motion

Edinburgh
The Salamander Press
1981

First published by The Salamander Press,
73 Morningside Park, Edinburgh EH10 5EZ.

ISBN 0 907540 05 8 (cloth)
ISBN 0 907540 06 6 (paper)

This edition consists of 1,800 *copies, of which* 600 *are casebound in cloth and* 1,200 *have paper covers.*

The author gratefully acknowledges the assistance of the Arts Council of Great Britain.

Set in Monotype Garamond by W. M. Bett Ltd.,
Lower Mill Street, Tillicoultry.
Printed by The Salamander Press, Edinburgh.
Bound by James, Joyce & Duffin Ltd.,
57 Ratcliffe Terrace, Edinburgh EH9 1SU.

A month home and awake
at three expecting light.
Still half the world in darkness
to roll away – but here I am

by the window, stooping,
quickly smearing a hole
in the misted silvery glass.
Your father's house,

his view of sand dunes
stubbled with grass, and the sea
heavily sliding, its craters split
and slammed shut to the moon.

As I look, wind staggers
the garden lilac, then races off
distressing the whole front –
the neighbour's gate squeaking

and banging, the pub-sign
knocking its frame once, twice,
and silent. But who is awake?
I glance at my bed and the sheet

thrown back, a crumpled ghost
where I slept – on the right,
as we did together. And there
with no more than the thought

I turn to the window again
and imagine you walking towards me –
in silence, bringing the friends,
the lost company, the servants I left,

everyone bowed and shawled
as though it were dawn, and this
wavering grey moonlight the dust
they had churned into early mist.

* * *

It was dawn when my journey finished
at last – three days, three nights stop-go
in my rickety Austin, a terrified
slow sweep from the Punjab down
past Delhi, Agra, Kanpur to reach

Kamaria: jumbled roofs and the sun
just clear into perfect blue. I drove
along sleeping streets, unshaven,
still scared. But no sign of the riots,
just slogans splashed and dribbling

Partition. No to Partition. Quit India.
What of my home? Would it be looted
by then? Or what? The manager's voice
came back to me over and over, blustering
Now we are free. No Britishers.

Now you must go – but smiling,
shaking my hand. Then I was home
and my servant ran to greet me
whispering *Go, sahib, It is dangerous.*
Go. All I could save was with me –

one suitcase, Shakespeare, a china mug
and the Hindustan Times, three days old.
I can see it now – your father's advertisement
circled with red ink, his name the friend
of a friend of a friend. In a week

when I stood in his narrow hall
for my interview, early, rehearsing my lines,
you were there. A sudden unthinking
surprised rush from your room, from a shower,
your hair darkened with water

and plastered down, your feet bare,
and one hand pulling the throat
of your dressing-gown close, hiding
the quick freckled blush I saw beginning
and deepening there like a burn.

* * *

So it began – our first blue midwinter.
Each cavernous cloudless morning
I drove to the godown at six

stocktaking wool for an hour:
indigo, crimson, natural, gold.
Then away round the villages –

Yes, I am new. Yes. Namaste.
The carpet sahib. Carpets –
and trained as an engineer . . .

House by house I ducked
and entered those close mud rooms.
The silences there. Fathers and sons

on their worn logs, smiling
through taut bars of string.
The twang and rustle of wool,

and the patterns rising.
Finish how soon? More smiles,
the waggling side-to-side head-shake,

Goodbye, and as evening approached
I circled back to my bungalow.
Would you be there? If I came

from Mirzapur, east, it was over
the high Ganges bridge. I would stop
midway, and leaning warily out

from the delicate parapet, whisper
your name *Let her love me.*
If not, let me not be found out.

Let her father like me. I waited
a moment, gazing down in the twilight,
then crumpled a single rupee note

and dropped it, straining to watch,
but never seeing the fall to its end
on the river's dark sluggish green.

* * *

It was our first time. We had shuffled
and clutched at club dances, and once
after tennis I kissed you, my hand
finding the warm small of your back,
brushing its damp soft hackle of hair.

Then it was midnight, and over the wall
I dropped down to the hushed MacFarlane garden –
your nervous adoring commando, crashing
and farcical. Which was your room?
Third right, in your letter. *Oh please,*

please come soon. I've been well
for at least ten days. My appendix is snug
in its jar on the window-sill, staring me out.
Your shutter unstuck with a parched squeak
Is it you? Yes. I kissed you again,

missing your mouth. *Ssssh.* The deliberate
firm tap-tapping of footsteps outside –
Nurse. Quick, in there, and I dragged
the heavy tallboy door shut behind me.
Your voices were hushed. *No, nothing*

thank you. Nothing. I'm fine. Good-night.
But I waited, your nightdresses hanging
close to my face, silky, and smelling of talc.
Then I was out. *Shoes off,* you said, *That's all,*
and I eased myself down on your narrow bed.

Careful! My stitches. Lie still,
still as you can. Like this. On your back.
And so you unbuttoned me,
gingerly kneeling astride, and then
with that gradual quickening dip and rise

you tipped evenly backwards and forwards
as if you were riding drunk – dissolving
the bed, the tallboy, the room, the dark coat
I ripped on the wall when I scrambled home
but wore unmended for days, as our secret sign.

* * *

Courting all that spring
to Independence – spring
and into the heat: shimmering days
I hurried to end for you.

Each late afternoon
we were side by side
at your father's bungalow,
longing for sunset, the punkah

lightly weighing us down
with its soft rush of air.
He smiled. *Really, you two.*
Go on . . . Supper's not yet . . .

and we were away, hand in hand
on the Austin's cracked back seat,
all windows down, the driver's face
staring ahead in the mirror.

They were perfect,
those cool evening drives:
the sun bleary with dust,
white eucalyptus avenues,

tiny flickering fires
and the sweet woodsmoke rising.
When will you marry me? Soon?
When you said it, you said it

lazily, breathing warm in my ear,
on that pot-holed road
out beyond Mirzapur. *Soon?*
We were late, with the engine off

at the crossing – a slender pole
waist high, and heat
still bouncing up from the rails,
warping the air. The keeper

emerged from his shack,
half lifted the pole,
listened, then slammed it back.
Up-down. Up-down you said, blushing,

and chafed my hand. We waited
in silence, hearing the train's deep
flustering *chomp*, *chomp* closer
and closer, a shrieking whistle,

and there it was. Benares –
Lahore on chipped plates,
windows barred, and the packed
vanishing faces of refugees.

* * *

Married in Independence week.
The factory shut, and the church
packed with the carpet wallahs
who caught us up in their holiday.
Now we are free, they were shouting,

Free – roping our necks with garlands
of roses and gainders. That night
before taking our honeymoon journey
north to the hills, we were secret
in Mirzapur's ramshackle best hotel,

strolling late round the pool.
A three foot scummy drop
to the water – its glassy length
steady and speckled with insects
performing their tiny pointless dance,

with the last swimmer long gone.
*I love you. Look at us. Husband
and wife* – you pointed down
at our faces, stared, and turned inside,
Come on – leaving your hand still grasped

in mine as we reached for the key
and the snub black light-switch.
Then you were screaming – *Let go.*
A furious quick sizzle. *Let go. Let go,*
and I did, with a sticky tear of skin.

We were driving at once, my good right hand
tight on the wheel, your left stretched
over, changing the gears to MacFarlane.
Back here – you said it teeth clenched
as we stood in the dark porch

side by side for a moment,
our hands stretched clear in front.
You nodded towards them – *Symbols?*
Symbols? Balls, I said, and smiled
leading you in. *Nurse. Hello. Are you there?*

*   *   *

A month alone
but stirring slowly, making
room in our lives for news

outside ourselves. Spring
brought the heat again – day
after day in my office the papers

built rustling under their weights,
shaken and plucked as the punkah
whipped round in its clammy rush.

On my wall I had pinned the first
free replacement map – India,
Pakistan: the new word jagged

up through the Indus valley to end
in the mountains' lumpy bruise.
When Gandhi died, your father

traced the frontier down
saying *Now. Now we shall see*,
and bowed his head, suddenly

homesick for England. Next day
he was round the villages talking,
cajoling, then back at my desk

empty-handed. *It's grief*, he said.
They won't do anything. You understand.
He stared at my map and sighed,

imagining high white cliffs
and gantries clearing through mist –
a dockside glossy with early rain.

*   *   *

With your father gone, and his furniture
gone or stacked in the godown waiting,
the house was ours. Tall white-washed rooms
and the spaces he left: dents in a carpet

for chairs, the crushed square of a cupboard.
Take care, he said, with his brave face
in the cabin doorway. *Remember*,
as soon as the baby comes, write.

Soon as you can. Now please . . . But we stayed
all morning, staring up from the quay, scanning
those tiny high rails for his wave
and seeing nothing, then nothing again

when he sailed, the liner unthinkably huge
as they tugged it clear, but suddenly
tiny – a slow dispersing feather
of smoke spiralling north. We imagined it

fading for days – free with ourselves
to ourselves at last. Each night
was our tender private game. *Listen.*
What can you hear? You would be lying back

with your dress pulled up, holding
my head side-on to your stomach. *Anything*?
Yes. I craned for the child's gurgle –
Yes. A boxer. That or a football player.

We slept outside that summer,
two wide-eyed effigies hand in hand
on the cool veranda, our hearts racing,
watching the stars blaze and swing

away through our nets. Five months,
six, and then for a week my trip alone
to Delhi on business. Should you have come?
Was that it? Even in summer? I travel

the last few miles of the journey back
endlessly. There is the taxi again
almost home from the station, and there
am I, with the windows wound right down

so my eyes run, blurring the house
and the one servant who met me.
Where is the memsahib? My question
returns off dazzling white walls. *Sahib*

he says, in a deep widening silence.
I remember cicadas, their manic bowing,
and sun crashing up from the yard,
then his voice breaks, *O Sahib*

and he turns towards me weeping.
But I am refusing to understand,
not moving, grinning, thinking of nothing
and letting the same unbidden phrase

occur to me over and over. *Sahib* –
he says it again. *I show you now.*
Humpti-tumpti gir giya phat.
Humpti-tumpti gir giya phat.

*   *   *

A scar of yellow clods.
The scratchmark of something
vanished. A dry scuffle.
You will wake up,
I was thinking, *Wake up,*

crouched with my head tilted
sideways as if I might
just make out your voice.
Sahib. It was the servant,
still weeping. *Baba too soon*

and bad. Like a snake.
I was hardly listening,
lost in the first moment
I brought you to life
underground: your hair set,

powder soft on your cheek,
and the dress slinking
back from your bare arms
as you stretch and show me
our slippery mottled child.

* * *

My solaces. The day's long
self-forgetting work, embarrassed
by those sad half-shouts
above the punkah whirring

Can I help you sahib?
Then evenings drunk alone –
the bedroom shutters drawn
and my shadow reeling to

and fro across their slats
folding dresses into tea-chests,
scooping up the baby-things,
your belts, a lacy petticoat,

shoes, blouses from the cupboard.
So much of you to find –
three nights but always something
overlooked, and then a fourth,

and rain. Almost home, I was
head-down through the yard
and stifling when it broke.
A long-drawn sizzling rip

like linen tearing, then
a pause and then the first
big drops distinct and smashed
in puffing spurts of dust.

Monsoon again. That night
I stretched across our bed
and drank among your last
unsorted clothes, the houselights

all turned off. No sleep,
but blankness interrupted
suddenly to find the rain
had quickened, thunder

cannoning above my roof,
the eucalyptus shimmering
and thrashed – its whole
enormous height smoking

in a constant crash.
Then blankness swimming back,
the rain dissolving,
and a dream releasing me

beyond my room, my garden,
bobbing on a grey race
of water to your grave.
I scrambled deep beside you

and was dry, tugging
at your clothes, whispering
Let go. Give me these
for laundry. Let them go.

* * *

How many days? Two, three, I let myself
sink from the world, half sleeping
or dreaming awake, with the rain
a steady hissing downpour, seething
to rot me through. When I first stood

outside in the glittering yard
it was morning. A week? More,
since you died? Nobody said –
it was all *Come here, sahib.*
Come quick, and someone splashing

ahead to the compound gates. *There.*
They waved one arm, its arc
sweeping the whole slope: *Ganga.*
I thought of your grave buried
deep underwater, and with it

the whole plain to my feet –
fields and dusty tracks lost
in a dimpled yellow-green lake
where bloated cattle were drifting
twice their size, gable-ends

jutted from froth, and the trees
had grown astonishing packages –
carpets rolled and strung above water,
their dark sacks a roost
for files of sodden ridiculous birds.

*   *   *

Now sit, sahib. Sit here.
It was the holy man,
patting the veranda floor.

Good. His face caked white
and crouching body
draped in a leopard skin –

a circus strongman
reading my life. *Sahib.*
You are an educate man.

Don't be afraid.
I am educate too: Hazlitt.
The beautiful lake poets.

You are lonely.
Eyes closed, and the greasy
ropes of hair. One hand pressing

down on his wire cage
and its parrot – a brilliant
green hat-feather tail.

You are lonely now.
His mesmerised voice
pausing, collecting itself.

You must go.
Your work here, finished.
The factory, finished,

his head leant sideways
and then *No more* –
almost a shout.

These are your own thoughts.
He was gone –
a faltering stooped prance

down to the yard, dragging
one leopard's foot in the dust.
Did I dream it?

Lying before me
were grains of wheat, a twig,
a charred thick chupatty.

* * *

My life out of my hands. By autumn
two perhaps three carpets a week.
Never enough. When I drove out
the weavers' houses were empty
ruinous shells, looms unstrung,

and everyone working all day in the fields,
shovelling grey Ganges silt into banks,
scraping and patting their ditches.
They will come back to us.
That was Pradeep, swirling his drink

as our final December AGM
dragged on. He frowned, *But when?*
They must care for their land . . .
then a shrug, and a blank stare
outside to the compound walls

and still eucalyptus trees.
We shall see. Yes, we shall see.
We spoke without thinking,
leaving the date of our sale
still vague as the evening darkened

and *Well*, said Pradeep, relieved
and embarrassed. *Well, we must finish.*
Time we should change. For the party
he meant – Mirzapur Christmas Dance
at the Club. By ten I was there, drunk

and hearing the Inkspots *Bless you*
for being an angel. Bless you for making
a new world just when the old world
crumbled so help-less-ly. The record
again and again like a commonplace

tender grief for that sweltering room
with its swathes of tinsel and ivy,
its yellow billiard cloths, and its walls
dotted with cotton-wool glued there
by servants who had never seen snow.

* * *

I woke at five to a bare house,
luggage already half way home.
My last morning: a delicate stripe
of sky strengthening under my door

and the chowkidar's shadowy steps
backwards and forwards, his cough,
and the phlegm with its soft scatter.
When I looked out he was gone –

his charpoy tipped to the wall,
and a torn-off tooth-brush stick
thrown on the balcony steps.
Sahib. A voice loud in the hall.

The driver's come.
I was bowed in the cold yard
as the servants draped their garlands on.
Roses and gainders – a necklace

of sweet-smelling tickling loops.
Goodbye, sahib. Goodbye. Goodbye.
I salaamed to the puckered faces,
not daring to speak, and was blind

through the compound gates and on
for a mile, two, of the dusty lane
until I leant forward. *Stop. Wait for me,*
wait, and I knelt at your grave.

Then the memory blurs. I can follow
my tentative hand to your stone,
touching as if it were braille –
Beloved wife. Their child,

but the images shift, and here I am
almost asleep at the window again,
smearing a hole in its misted
silvery glass. There are footsteps now –

your father's, crossing the landing.
He calls to me, *Seven o'clock*,
and clumps downstairs. I watch
a whining milkfloat clatter house

by house down the street,
and daylight begin. The sun is no more
than a thin whitening slit. The sea
a bleak horizon returning to grey.